Unleashing the Power of DAX:

Beginner to Advanced Techniques for Power BI

Contents

Introduction

Welcome to " Unleashing the Power of DAX: Beginner to Advanced Techniques for Power BI" In this book, we will dive into the world of advanced DAX (Data Analysis Expressions) formulas and explore powerful techniques to take your Power BI skills to the next level.

Power BI has revolutionized the way organizations analyze and visualize data, enabling them to make informed business decisions. While the basics of DAX are widely covered in various learning resources, this book aims to go beyond the fundamentals and provide you with a comprehensive understanding of advanced DAX tricks that are not commonly found in books.

Throughout the chapters, we will explore a wide range of advanced DAX formulas and their application in real-world business scenarios. Each chapter will delve into a specific topic, providing detailed explanations, practical examples, and step-by-step guides to reinforce your learning. Whether you are a data analyst, business intelligence professional, or Power BI enthusiast, this book will equip you with the knowledge and skills to tackle complex data challenges and unlock valuable insights.

1   How to Connect Data to Power BI

1.1   Open Power BI Desktop

When you open Power BI Desktop, a welcome screen appears. From this screen, you can connect to data, open existing reports, and get help with Power BI. If you want to connect to data right away, select the 'Get Data' button on the welcome screen.

1.2   Select Your Data Source

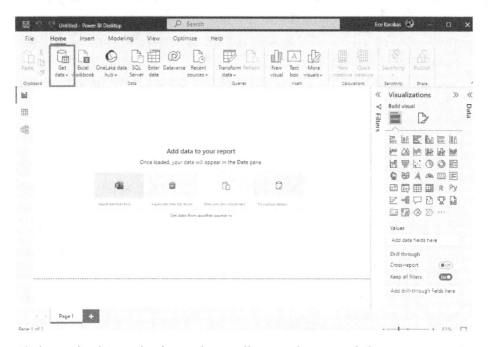

Click on the 'Home' tab on the toolbar at the top of the screen, and then click on the 'Get Data' button. You'll see a list of all the different types of data sources you can connect to. Power BI can connect to many different types of data, including Excel files, SQL Server databases, SharePoint lists, Salesforce reports, and many others. You'll need to select the type that corresponds to your data source.

1.3 Connect to Your Data Source

Once you've selected your data source, you'll need to provide the information necessary to connect to it. This can vary depending on the type of data source.

For example, if you're connecting to an Excel file, you'll need to navigate to the location of the file on your computer or network. If you're connecting to a SQL Server database, you'll need to provide the server name, database name, and your credentials (username and password). If you are connecting Sharepoint Excel, you'll need to have sharepoint list url, and from this link you can select your Excel file.

1.4 Select Your Data

After you've connected to your data source, you'll be able to select the data that you want to use in your report. If you're connecting to a file, you'll see a preview of the data in the file. If you're connecting to a database or other large data source, you might only see a list of tables or views. Select the ones that contain the data you want to use, and then click 'Load'

1.5   Transform Your Data (Optional)

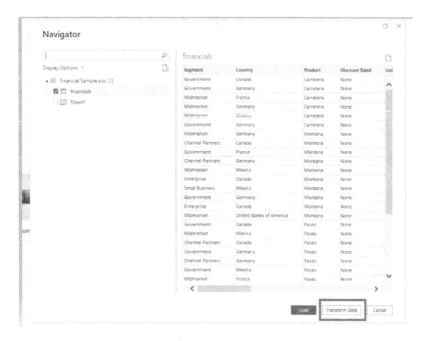

Before you load your data, you might want to transform it. Power BI's Query Editor allows you to clean and transform data before loading it. You can remove unnecessary columns, change data types, create calculated columns, and more. If you want to do this, click 'Edit' instead of 'Load' after selecting your data. Once you've finished transforming your data, click 'Close & Apply' in the Query Editor to load your data.

1.6   Load Your Data

Once you've selected and optionally transformed your data, it will be loaded into Power BI and you'll be able to start creating your report. The fields from your data will appear in the Fields pane on the right side of the screen, and you can drag and drop them onto the report canvas to start creating visualizations.

Remember, connecting to data in Power BI is just the first step. The real power of Power BI comes from using this data to create insightful, interactive reports and dashboards. Spend some time learning about Power BI's visualization tools to make the most of your data. Introduction to DAX syntax and formula structure.

After loading your data you can go to Query, and check the "Column Quality" from openning View tab and clicking column quality option. This helps us the check the errors and empty cells from our source data.

Then let's save and close the Query.

2 Creating a Report

2.1 Choosing Fields

After loading data, in the Fields pane, you can drag and drop the fields onto the main canvas to create your first visualization. For example, if you have sales data, you could drag the "Sales" field to the Values area and "Country" to the Axis area to create a bar chart of sales by region.

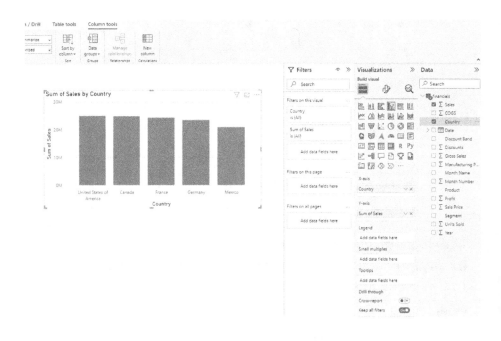

2.2   Choosing Visualization Type

The type of visualization can be changed using the Visualization pane. Here, you have the default options like bar charts, column charts, line charts, pie charts, maps, and many others. The choice should depend on the kind of data you are working with and what you want to express. You can always search for new visuals from the three dots at the end of Visualizations.

2.3   Customizing Visualizations

When a visualization is selected, the Visualization pane changes to allow different fields to be added or removed from the current visualization. You can also adjust the aggregation (sum, average, count, etc.)   of   each   field   here.

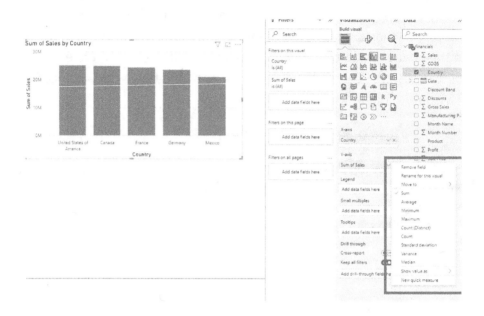

2.4 Formatting the Report

In the Format tab, you can change the colors, add data labels, change the font size and styles, and much more to enhance the visual appeal and clarity of your report. Also, the report page can be formatted to add a page background, change the page size, and so on.

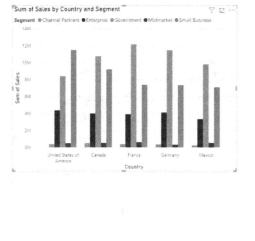

3 Creating a Dashboard

3.1 Pinning Visuals

Once you're satisfied with your report, you can create a dashboard by pinning visuals. Hover over the visual and click the pin icon. You'll be prompted to choose a dashboard, where you can either select an existing one or create a new one.

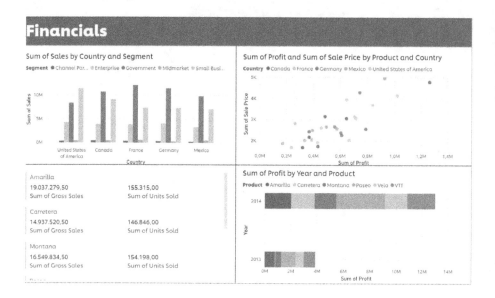

3.2 Arranging Dashboard Tiles

Once on the dashboard, each visualization appears as a tile. You can rearrange the tiles, resize them, and further customize how your dashboard looks to provide a high-level view of your data.

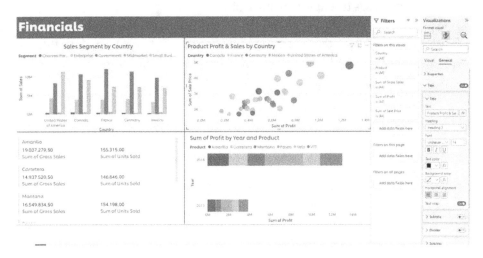

You can do all changes by clicking the visual you want to update and go to "Visualizations" section, click on the Formatting tab. You we will be able to change all the visual appreances from here.

3.3   Using Q&A to Explore Your Data

Power BI dashboards offer a Q&A feature where you can type in questions related to your data, and Power BI will generate visuals to answer them. It's a powerful way to explore data.

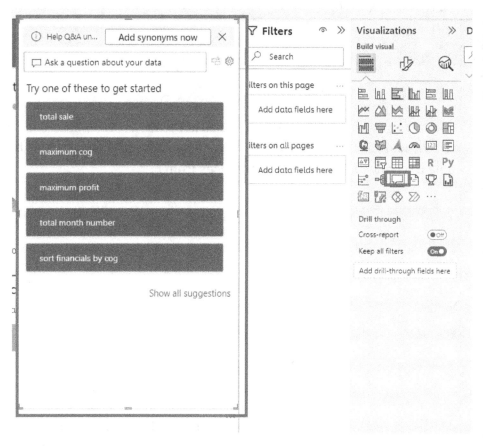

By clicking the up setting icon of Q&A, we will be able to customize this function such as,

Adding synonyms, Review Questions, Teach the Q&A about the questions that users my have and also Suggest some other questions.

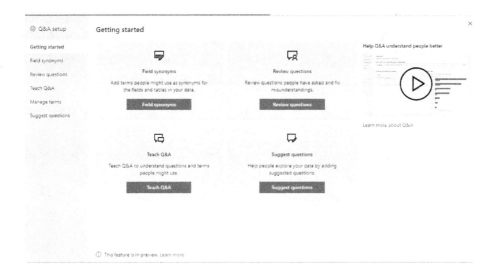

4 How to Auto-Create with PowerBI

Power BI provides a feature called "Auto Create", which simplifies the process of creating visualizations based on the data you have imported. It uses artificial intelligence to identify patterns and meaningful relationships in your data to automatically create a collection of visuals, which are organized into a report.

Here's a detailed guide on how to use the "Auto Create" feature:

As a first step we will need to open the webpage of PowerBI; https://app.powerbi.com/home?experience=power-bi

Then we have to click on the "+" button on left pane. Then we will selet the "Paste or Manually Enter Data" option.

4.1 Upload Your Data

Log into Power BI web service (app.powerbi.com). On the left-hand sidebar, you can select 'Datasets'. Here, you have the option to 'Get Data'. Click on this, and you'll be directed to a new page. You can then select 'Files' from the list of options to upload your data. Power BI supports Excel workbooks, Power BI Desktop files, and CSV files.

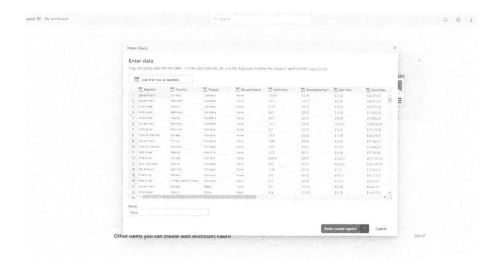

After uploading the data, click on "Auto-create Report" option.

4.2 Use Auto Create

After your dataset has been uploaded and processed, find it in the 'Datasets' section. Hover over the dataset and click on the 'More options' button (three dots). From the menu that appears, select 'Auto Create'.

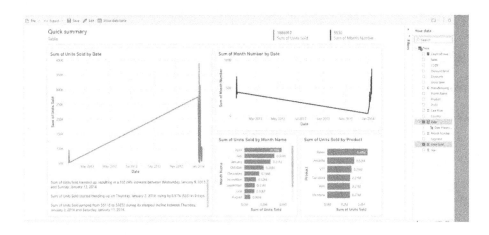

4.3　Customize Your Report

The 'Auto Create' feature is a great starting point, but you may want to customize the report to better suit your needs.

And for additional information, filtering or customizing you can always edit your dashboard by clicking "Edit" option on the top task bar or you can download the prepared dashboard from "Files" -> "Download a Copy" option and resume your editing from there.

PowerBI has a "Smart Narrative" visual option which enables to auto creat comments about your data usign AI. You can see the visual on left down below.

4.4　Review Your Report

Power BI will then start analyzing your data, looking for trends, outliers, and correlations. This process can take a few minutes. Once completed, Power BI will present you with a report consisting of various charts, graphs, and tables. This report is generated based on what Power BI's algorithms determine to be the most interesting and relevant insights from your data.

4.5　Save and Share Your Report

Once you're happy with your report, don't forget to save it. You can then share it with others in your organization by clicking on the 'Share' button at the top of the screen.

Please note that 'Auto Create' may not always create the exact report you want, and it's not a substitute for understanding your data and the capabilities of Power BI. However, it's a great tool for quickly generating a starting point for your data exploration, especially when you're dealing with a new dataset or you're not sure what insights might be hidden in your data.

5   Measure and Calculated Columns

Understanding the difference between Measures and Calculated Columns in Power BI is important. They both allow you to add new data to your model, but they work in fundamentally different ways and serve different purposes.

5.1   Calculated Columns

A Calculated Column is a column that you add to an existing table in the data model. It uses a DAX formula that is applied to every row in the column, and the result of this formula is stored in the data model. This means that a calculated column takes up space in memory.

For example, suppose you have a sales table with 'Units Sold' and 'Price per Unit' columns. You could create a calculated column named 'Total Sales', using the formula [Units Sold] * [Price per Unit]. This will calculate the total sales for each row in the table.

Calculated columns are useful when you want to slice and dice on the calculated result or when you want to use the result of a calculation in another calculation that aggregates the result further.

5.2 Measures

A Measure, on the other hand, is a calculation that is performed on the fly as you interact with your reports. It uses a DAX formula that can aggregate data based on your current context. The result isn't stored in the data model, it's calculated in real time based on your current filters and selections.

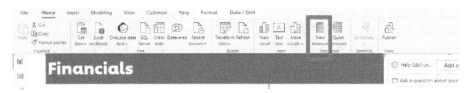

Continuing with the previous example, you could create a measure named 'Total Sales' using the formula SUMX('Sales', [Units Sold] * [Price per Unit]). This would sum up the total sales for all the rows in the Sales table that meet the current filter conditions.

Measures are particularly useful when you want to perform calculations that need to adjust dynamically as you slice and dice your data or when you want to perform complex aggregations such as averages, percentages, or calculations that involve several different tables.

5.3 Summary

In essence, the key difference between calculated columns and measures comes down to when and how the calculations are made, as well as how they are used. Calculated columns are calculated when the data is loaded and take up space in memory, and they can be used like any other column in your data. Measures are calculated on the fly and are mainly used in visuals, not in the rows of tables.

Choosing whether to use a calculated column or a measure will depend on your specific needs and how you want to use the result of your calculation.

6 Operators

Power BI has a variety of operators that fall into different categories, including arithmetic, comparison, text, and logical operators. These operators can be used in DAX formulas, which is the formula language used in Power BI.

6.1 Arithmetic Operators

These operators are used to perform basic mathematical operations:

Addition (+): Adds two numbers. Example: Column1 + Column2

Subtraction (-): Subtracts the second number from the first. Example: Column1 - Column2

Multiplication (*): Multiplies two numbers. Example: Column1 * Column2

Division (/): Divides the first number by the second. Example: Column1 / Column2

Exponentiation (^): Raises the first number to the power of the second. Example: Column1 ^ Column2

6.2 Comparison Operators

Comparison operators are used to compare two values:

Equal to (=): Checks if two values are equal. Example: Column1 = Column2

Not equal to (<>): Checks if two values are not equal. Example: Column1 <> Column2

Greater than (>): Checks if the first value is greater than the second. Example: Column1 > Column2

Less than (<): Checks if the first value is less than the second. Example: Column1 < Column2

Greater than or equal to (>=): Checks if the first value is greater than or equal to the second. Example: Column1 >= Column2

Less than or equal to (<=): Checks if the first value is less than or equal to the second. Example: Column1 <= Column2

6.3   Text Operators

Text operators are used to manipulate strings of text:

Concatenation (&): Combines two text strings into one. Example: "First Name" & "Last Name"

Logical Operators

Logical operators are used to perform logical operations, typically with boolean (TRUE or FALSE) values:

And (&&): Returns TRUE if both conditions are TRUE. Example: Column1 > 20 && Column2 < 30

Or (||): Returns TRUE if either or both conditions are TRUE. Example: Column1 > 20 || Column2 < 30

Not (!): Returns the opposite of a boolean value. Example: ! (Column1 > 20)

When creating complex expressions in DAX, these operators can be combined. Understanding how to use them is essential to harnessing the full power of Power BI for data analysis. Always remember to carefully manage the precedence of operators to ensure that calculations are performed in the correct order.

7 Deep-Dive to DAX

DAX, which stands for Data Analysis Expressions, is a collection of functions, operators, and constants that can be used in formulas or expressions in Power BI, Analysis Services, and Power Pivot in Excel. Let's deep dive into a few DAX formulas:

7.1 SUM() Function:

SUM is a very common function used in DAX and it does exactly what you'd expect - it adds up the numbers in a column.

For instance, if you have a column named SalesAmount in a table named Sales, you could calculate the total sales with the following formula:

```
TotalSales = SUM(Sales[SalesAmount])
```

7.2 AVERAGE() Function:

This function returns the arithmetic mean of a set of values in a column.

Let's say you have a column ProductRating in a table Products, the average product rating can be calculated like this:

```
Average Product Rating = AVERAGE(Products[ProductRating])
```

7.3 COUNT() Function:

The COUNT function returns the number of items in a set. For instance, if you want to count the number of sales transactions:

```
Number of Transactions = COUNT(Sales[TransactionID])
```

7.4 CALCULATE() Function:

The CALCULATE function is one of the most powerful and versatile functions in DAX. It allows you to modify the context under which a calculation is made.

For example, you could calculate the total sales for a specific region (let's say "West") like this:

```
Total Sales West Region = CALCULATE(SUM(Sales[SalesAmount]), Sales[Region] = "West")
```

7.5 CONCATENATEX() Function:

This function joins two text strings into one text string. It's helpful when you want to combine text from multiple rows of data into a single, comma-separated value.

For instance, if you have a table Customers and you want to create a list of all customer names:

```
Customer        List        =           CONCATENATEX(Customers,
Customers[CustomerName], ", ")
```

7.6   RELATED() Function:

The RELATED function is used when you want to bring related data from another table into the current table. It's helpful when your data model has relationships between tables.

For instance, if you have a Sales table and a Products table, and you want to add the product name to the sales table:

```
Product Name = RELATED(Products[ProductName])
```

7.7   DISTINCTCOUNT() Function:

This function returns the count of distinct values in a column.

For example, if you want to count the distinct number of products sold:

```
Distinct        Products        Sold        =
DISTINCTCOUNT(Sales[ProductID])
```

7.8   MAX() and MIN() Functions:

The MAX function returns the maximum value in a column, while the MIN function returns the minimum value in a column.

For example, to find the most expensive and cheapest products sold:

```
Max Price = MAX(Sales[Price])
Min Price = MIN(Sales[Price])
```

7.9 DIVIDE() Function:

The DIVIDE function performs division and handles errors when you divide by zero.

For example, to calculate the average price per unit:

```
Average        Price        Per        Unit        =
DIVIDE(SUM(Sales[TotalPrice]),
SUM(Sales[Quantity]))
```

7.10 EARLIER() Function:

The EARLIER function is a very useful DAX function when you want to use a certain value as input to all rows of the table where the expression is being calculated, but the value might vary for each row calculation. This is particularly useful when calculating running totals.

For example, to calculate a running total of sales:

```
Running Total =
CALCULATE (
    SUM ( Sales[SalesAmount] ),
    FILTER (
        ALL ( Sales ),
        Sales[OrderDate]        <=        EARLIER        (
Sales[OrderDate] )
    )
)
```

7.11 RANKX() Function:

The RANKX function returns the rank of a number in a list of numbers for each row in the table argument.

For example, to get the sales rank of each product based on the total sales:

```
Sales Rank = RANKX(ALL(Sales[ProductID]), [Total
Sales])
```

7.12 ALL(), ALLEXCEPT() Functions:

ALL returns all the rows in a table, or all the values in a column, ignoring any filters that might have been applied. ALLEXCEPT returns all the rows in a table except for those rows that are affected by the specified column filters.

For instance, to calculate the percentage of total sales for each product:

```
Percentage of Total Sales = DIVIDE([Total Sales],
CALCULATE([Total Sales], ALL(Sales))) * 100
```

7.13 SWITCH() Function:

The SWITCH function returns different results depending on the value of an expression.

For example, to categorize sales into different levels based on their value:

```
Sales Level = SWITCH(
    TRUE(),
    [Total Sales] < 10000, "Low",
    [Total Sales] < 50000, "Medium",
    "High"
)
```

In this case, if total sales are less than 10,000, it's classified as "Low". If it's between 10,000 and 50,000, it's "Medium". Otherwise, it's "High".

7.14 CALCULATETABLE() Function:

CALCULATETABLE modifies the context in which a table expression is evaluated.

For instance, if you want to create a table of all the "High" level sales:

```
High Sales = CALCULATETABLE(
    Sales,
    Sales[Sales Level] = "High"
)
```

7.15 SAMEPERIODLASTYEAR() Function:

This function returns a set of dates in the current selection for the same period last year.

For example, to calculate sales for the same period in the previous year:

```
Sales Previous Year = CALCULATE(
    SUM(Sales[SalesAmount]),
    SAMEPERIODLASTYEAR('Date'[Date])
)
```

7.16 YEAR(), MONTH(), DAY() Functions:

These functions extract the year, month, and day from a date, respectively.

For example, to extract the year from a 'Date' column:

```
Year = YEAR(Sales[Date])
```

7.17 DATEDIFF() Function:

This function returns the count of interval boundaries crossed between two dates.

For example, to calculate the number of days between the order date and ship date:

```
Days to Ship = DATEDIFF(Sales[OrderDate],
Sales[ShipDate],                          DAY)
```

7.18 BLANK() Function:

The BLANK function returns a blank. This is useful for handling null or missing values.

For instance, if you want to replace null values in the 'Discount' column with 0:

```
Discount    =    IF(ISBLANK(Sales[Discount]),    0,
Sales[Discount])
```

7.19 SUMX() and AVERAGEX() Functions:

These functions are variations of the SUM() and AVERAGE() functions. They iterate over a table and evaluate an expression for each row before aggregating the results.

For instance, to calculate total sales where the calculation for each row is [Units Sold] * [Price per Unit]:

```
Total Sales = SUMX(Sales, Sales[Units Sold] *
Sales[Price per Unit])
```

7.20 FILTER() Function:

The FILTER function returns a table that has been filtered to include or exclude certain rows.

For example, to create a new table that includes only 'High' sales:

```
High Sales = FILTER(Sales, Sales[Sales Level] =
"High")
```

7.21 ALLSELECTED() Function:

The ALLSELECTED function returns all the rows in a table that are currently active or selected, based on any slicer or filter that has been applied.

For instance, to calculate the total sales for all selected regions:

```
Total Sales Selected Regions =
CALCULATE(SUM(Sales[SalesAmount]),
ALLSELECTED(Sales[Region]))
```

7.22 RANK.EQ() Function:

The RANK.EQ function returns the rank of a number in a list of numbers. The ".EQ" part means that it handles ties by giving them the same rank.

For example, to calculate the rank of each product by sales:

```
Sales Rank = RANK.EQ(Sales[Total Sales],
ALLSELECTED(Sales[Total Sales]))
```

7.23 RELATEDTABLE() Function:

The RELATEDTABLE function gives you a table that includes all the rows that have a relationship with the current row.

For example, if you have a 'Customers' table and an 'Orders' table, and you want to get all the orders for a specific customer:

```
Customer Orders = RELATEDTABLE(Orders)
```

7.24 ISINSCOPE() Function:

The ISINSCOPE function checks if a column is currently being used in a visual. This can be useful for creating measures that behave differently in different visuals.

For example, to calculate total sales, but to return BLANK() if the 'Region' column is in scope:

```
Total Sales = IF(ISINSCOPE(Sales[Region]), BLANK(),
SUM(Sales[SalesAmount]))
```

7.25 GENERATE() and GENERATEALL() Functions:

These functions are used to create a cartesian product between each row from two tables.

For example, if you want to create a table with each combination of 'Product' and 'Region':

```
Product Region Combinations = GENERATE(Products,
Regions)
```

7.26 HASONEVALUE() Function:

This function returns true when the specified column has exactly one distinct value.

For instance, to check if only one product is selected in a filter:

```
Is One Product Selected =
HASONEVALUE(Products[Product])
```

7.27   UNION(), INTERSECT(), and EXCEPT() Functions:

These functions allow you to perform set operations on tables. UNION combines two tables into one, INTERSECT returns only the rows that appear in both tables, and EXCEPT returns only the rows from the first table that don't appear in the second.

For example, to create a table that includes customers who bought both 'Product A' and 'Product B':

```
Customers of A and B =
INTERSECT(
    CALCULATETABLE(Customers,    Sales[Product]    =
"Product A"),
    CALCULATETABLE(Customers,    Sales[Product]    =
"Product B")
)
```

7.28   FORMAT() Function:

The FORMAT function allows you to convert a value to a text according to a specified format.

For instance, to format 'SalesDate' as 'Month-Year':

```
Formatted Date = FORMAT(Sales[SalesDate], "MM-yyyy")
```

7.29 USERELATIONSHIP() Function:

When you have multiple relationships between two tables, Power BI will only use one as the 'Active' relationship. The USERELATIONSHIP function allows you to specify a different relationship to be used in a specific calculation.

For example, if you have a 'Sales' table and a 'Dates' table with two relationships - 'Order Date' and 'Ship Date':

```
Total Sales by Ship Date =
CALCULATE(
    SUM(Sales[SalesAmount]),
    USERELATIONSHIP(Sales[ShipDate], Dates[Date])
)
```

7.30 XIRR() Function:

The XIRR function returns the internal rate of return for a schedule of cash flows that is not necessarily periodic.

For example, if you have an 'Investments' table with 'CashFlow' and 'Date' columns:

```
Investment IRR = XIRR(Investments[CashFlow], Investments[Date])
```

7.31 EVALUATE Statement:

In DAX, the EVALUATE statement is used to run a query against the data model. You can use it to test your measures and calculated columns, and it's crucial when you're using DAX in an environment like SQL Server Analysis Services (SSAS) or Power Pivot.

For example, if you want to see a list of customers and their respective total   sales:

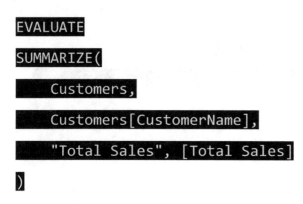

```
EVALUATE
SUMMARIZE(
    Customers,
    Customers[CustomerName],
    "Total Sales", [Total Sales]
)
```

7.32 CROSSJOIN() Function:

The CROSSJOIN function generates a cartesian product of all rows from all tables in the table arguments.

For instance, to generate all possible combinations of 'Product' and 'Region':

```
Product Region Combinations = CROSSJOIN(Products,
Regions)
```

7.33 Variables in DAX:

You can use the VAR keyword to create a new variable in a DAX expression, which can make your code cleaner and more efficient.

For example, to calculate the profit margin for each product:

```
Profit Margin =
VAR TotalCost = SUMX(Sales, Sales[Units Sold] *
Sales[Cost per Unit])
VAR TotalRevenue = SUMX(Sales, Sales[Units Sold] *
Sales[Price per Unit])
RETURN    DIVIDE(TotalRevenue    -    TotalCost,
TotalRevenue)
```

7.34 CALCULATE vs CALCULATETABLE Functions:

CALCULATE and CALCULATETABLE are similar but used in different contexts. CALCULATE modifies the context in which a scalar expression is evaluated, while CALCULATETABLE modifies the context in which a table expression is evaluated.

For instance, to calculate the average sales only for 'Product A':

```
Average          Sales          Product          A          =
CALCULATE(AVERAGE(Sales[SalesAmount]),
Sales[Product]          =          "Product          A")
```

7.35 KEEPFILTERS Function:

The KEEPFILTERS function changes the context transition behavior of a CALCULATE/CALCULATETABLE function by preserving any existing filters in the filter context.

For instance, if you have two slicers on a report – one for 'Region' and one for 'Product', and you want a measure to respect both slicers:

```
Total   Sales   =   CALCULATE(SUM(Sales[SalesAmount]),
KEEPFILTERS(Values(Sales[Region])),
KEEPFILTERS(Values(Sales[Product])))
```

7.36 PATH(), PATHLENGTH(), PATHITEM(), PATHITEMREVERSE(), PATHCONTAINS() Functions:

These functions allow you to work with hierarchies and parent-child relationships in your data. For example, you can use these functions to analyze data that is organized in a tree structure.

For example, if you have a 'Employees' table that has 'EmployeeID' and 'ManagerID', you can use these functions to construct an organizational chart, calculate the distance between two employees in the hierarchy, or check if one employee is a subordinate of another.

7.37 EARLIER() Function:

The EARLIER() function is a tricky function to understand, but it's incredibly useful. It returns the value of the specified column for a row that is "earlier" in the DAX execution sequence. This can be useful in calculations that require a row to be compared to previous rows in the table.

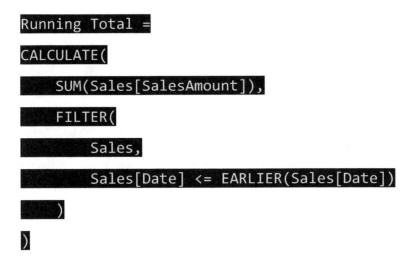

```
Running Total =
CALCULATE(
    SUM(Sales[SalesAmount]),
    FILTER(
        Sales,
        Sales[Date] <= EARLIER(Sales[Date])
    )
)
```

This example calculates a running total of sales. The FILTER function uses EARLIER to get all the rows where the date is earlier or equal to the date in the current row.

7.38 RANKX() Function:

The RANKX function can be used to rank values in your data. It returns the rank of a number in a list of numbers for each row in the table argument.

```
Sales Rank =
RANKX(
    ALL(Sales[Product]),
    CALCULATE(SUM(Sales[SalesAmount]))
)
```

This example calculates a sales rank for each product. The RANKX function ranks each product based on the sum of sales for that product.

7.39 ALLSELECTED() Function in Advanced Context:

This function is often used in conjunction with other functions to modify the context of a calculation. It returns all the rows in a table, or all the values in a column, ignoring any filters that might have been applied inside the query, but keeping filters that come from outside.

This example calculates the percentage of total sales that each row represents, based on the currently selected filters.

7.40 Advanced Time Intelligence:

Time intelligence functions are used to create calculations over periods of time. Examples of these functions include TOTALYTD(), SAMEPERIODLASTYEAR(), and DATESBETWEEN(). To use these functions correctly, you need a separate date table that isn't filtered and that covers the whole range of dates in your data.

```
YoY Growth =
DIVIDE(
    SUM(Sales[SalesAmount])                                    -
CALCULATE(SUM(Sales[SalesAmount]),
SAMEPERIODLASTYEAR('Date'[Date])),
    CALCULATE(SUM(Sales[SalesAmount]),
SAMEPERIODLASTYEAR('Date'[Date]))
)
```

This example calculates the year-over-year growth in sales.

7.41 CONTAINS() Function:

This function checks whether the rows of a table contain a specific value at a column.

```
Is    There    a    Discount    =    CONTAINS(Orders,
Orders[Discount],                                    ">0")
```

7.42 Complex Relationships:

There can be multiple relationships between two tables in Power BI. By default, only one of them is active and used in calculations, but you can use the USERELATIONSHIP function to specify another one.

```
Total Sales = CALCULATE(
    SUM('Sales'[SalesAmount]),
```

```
    USERELATIONSHIP('Sales'[OrderDate],
'Date'[Date])

)
```

This DAX expression calculates the total sales based on the order date, even if the active relationship is based on the shipping date.

7.43 Semi-Additive Measures:

Some measures, like inventory levels or account balances, are not additive across time – the typical aggregation you might want to do for such a measure is to take the last value. The LASTNONBLANK and FIRSTNONBLANK functions are used in such cases.

```
End of Month Inventory = CALCULATE(

    SUM('Inventory'[InventoryLevel]),

    LASTNONBLANK('Date'[Date],
'Inventory'[InventoryLevel])

)
```

This DAX expression calculates the inventory level at the end of each month.

These are some of the more complex topics you might face in DAX. As always, the key to mastering DAX is understanding your data and the logic behind each function, and practicing with real-world scenarios.

8 DAX Optimization

8.1 Identifying performance bottlenecks in DAX formulas

This section focuses on techniques to identify performance issues in DAX formulas. The example provided demonstrates evaluating the performance of a SUMX calculation on the Sales table. issues:

```
Evaluate SUMX(
    Sales,
    Sales[Quantity] * Sales[UnitPrice]
)
```

8.2 Techniques to optimize complex calculations:

This section covers strategies for optimizing complex DAX calculations. The first example showcases simplifying a complex calculation by using the SUMX function on the Sales table. The second example demonstrates using CALCULATETABLE instead of FILTER for improved performance.

Example of using CALCULATETABLE instead of FILTER:

```
TotalSales    =    CALCULATE(SUM(Sales[SalesAmount]),
CALCULATETABLE(Sales, Sales[Year] = 2022))
```

8.3 Leveraging query folding and query performance

This subsection explains the significance of query folding in Power BI and how it impacts performance. The example demonstrates optimizing data sources and utilizing query folding to enhance performance.

Example of optimizing data sources and query folding:

```
EVALUATE SUMMARIZECOLUMNS(
    'Sales'[Product],
    'Sales'[Country],
    'Sales'[Year],
    "TotalSales", SUM('Sales'[SalesAmount])
)
```

8.4 Profiling DAX formulas for improved efficiency

This subsection explores the use of DAX Studio, a tool for profiling and analyzing DAX formula performance. The example showcases defining a measure and evaluating its result using DAX Studio.

Example of using DAX Studio for profiling DAX formulas:

```
DEFINE
                MEASURE     Sales[TotalSales]     =
SUM(Sales[SalesAmount])
EVALUATE
    ROW("Result", Sales[TotalSales])
```

9 Advanced Table Relationships

9.1 Understanding advanced relationship types

This section delves into different types of relationships in Power BI, such as one-to-one and one-to-many. The example provides a simple representation of a one-to-one relationship between the Sales and Customers tables.

Example of one-to-one relationship:

```
Sales[SalesOrderLineID]               ->          Sales
Order[SalesOrderLineID]
```

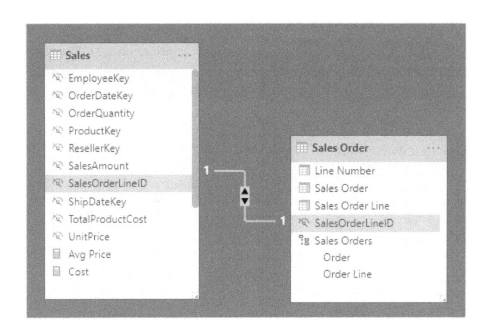

Example of one-to-many relationship:

`Stores[stor_id] -> Sales[store_id]`

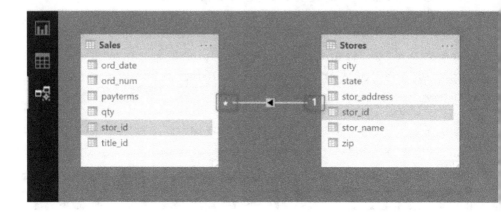

9.2   Implementing many-to-many relationships

This subsection focuses on many-to-many relationships and explains the usage of bridge tables. The example illustrates a many-to-many relationship between the Sales, OrderDetails, and Products tables.

Example of many-to-many relationship using bridge table:

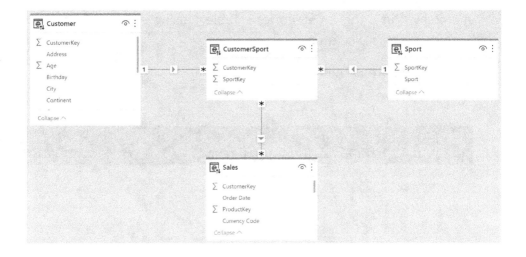

9.3 Solving circular dependencies and ambiguity

This subsection addresses circular dependencies and ambiguity in table relationships. The example presents a circular relationship between three tables and emphasizes the need for resolution to avoid conflicts.

Example of circular dependency resolution:

```
TableA[ColumnA] -> TableB[ColumnB]
TableB[ColumnB] -> TableC[ColumnC]
TableC[ColumnC] -> TableA[ColumnA]
```

9.4 Hierarchical relationships and parent-child hierarchies

This subsection discusses hierarchical relationships and parent-child hierarchies in table structures. The example showcases a parent-child hierarchy in the Categories table using CategoryID and ParentCategoryID columns.

Example of parent-child hierarchy:

```
Categories[CategoryID]                                        ->
Categories[ParentCategoryID]
```

10 Advanced Calculations with Variables

10.1 Declaring and using variables in DAX formulas

This section introduces the concept of variables in DAX and how they can be used in formulas. The example demonstrates declaring variables for DiscountedRevenue and TaxRate to calculate TotalRevenue.

Example of declaring and using variables:

```
TotalRevenue =
VAR DiscountedRevenue = [Revenue] * 0.9
VAR TaxRate = 0.2
RETURN
    DiscountedRevenue * (1 - TaxRate)
```

10.2 Creating dynamic measures and calculations

This subsection explores the creation of dynamic measures based on user selections. The example showcases the use of the SWITCH function to create a dynamic measure based on the selected value from a MeasureSelector table.

Example of creating dynamic measures:

```
SelectedMeasure =
    SWITCH(
        SELECTEDVALUE('MeasureSelector'[Measure]),
```

```
      "TotalSales", [TotalSales],
      "ProfitMargin", [ProfitMargin]
  )
```

10.3 Improving code readability and maintainability

This subsection emphasizes the importance of code readability and maintainability. The example demonstrates improving code readability by using variables to store intermediate results in the TotalSales calculation.

Example of improving code readability with variables:

```
TotalSales =
VAR UnitPrice = SUM(Sales[UnitPrice])
VAR Quantity = SUM(Sales[Quantity])
RETURN
    UnitPrice * Quantity
```

10.4 Leveraging variable scope and context

This subsection explains variable scope and how it affects calculations. The example showcases the usage of variables with different scopes to calculate TotalRevenue based on RegionRevenue and CountryRevenue.

Example of leveraging variable scope:

```
TotalRevenue =
VAR RegionRevenue = CALCULATE(SUM(Sales[Revenue]),
Sales[Region] = "North")
```

```
VAR CountryRevenue = CALCULATE(SUM(Sales[Revenue]),
Sales[Country] = "USA")
RETURN
    RegionRevenue + CountryRevenue
```

11 Advanced Time Intelligence

11.1 Customizing time intelligence calculations:

This chapter delves into advanced time intelligence calculations and how they can be customized for specific business needs. Examples will include calculations like Year-to-Date (YTD), Quarter-to-Date (QTD), Month-to-Date (MTD), and rolling averages.

Example of YTD calculation:

```
TotalSalesYTD = TOTALYTD(SUM(Sales[SalesAmount]),
Dates[Date])
```

In this example, the TOTALYTD function is used to calculate the total sales amount from the beginning of the year to the selected date.

11.2 Handling non-standard fiscal calendars:

This section focuses on scenarios where the fiscal calendar doesn't align with the standard calendar. It covers techniques to handle non-standard fiscal calendars and adjust time intelligence calculations accordingly.

Example of adjusting time intelligence calculations for a non-standard fiscal calendar:

```
TotalSalesQTD   =   TOTALQTD(SUM(Sales[SalesAmount]),
Dates[Date], 0, "FiscalYearStartMonth")
```

In this example, the TOTALQTD function is used to calculate the quarter-to-date sales amount based on a non-standard fiscal calendar where the fiscal year starts from a specific month.

11.3   Calculating rolling averages and moving totals:

This subsection explores calculating rolling averages and moving totals over a specified period. It demonstrates the use of functions like AVERAGEX and SUMX combined with DATESINPERIOD to compute rolling averages and moving totals.

Example of calculating a rolling average:

```
RollingAverage =
DIVIDE(
    SUMX(Sales, Sales[SalesAmount]),
                COUNTROWS(DATESINPERIOD(Dates[Date],
LASTDATE(Dates[Date]), -30, DAY))
)
```

In this example, the rolling average is calculated by summing the sales amount over the last 30 days and dividing it by the number of days in the period.

12 Advanced Statistical Analysis

12.1 Statistical calculations in DAX:

This chapter focuses on performing advanced statistical calculations using DAX. It covers functions like AVERAGEX, STDEV.P, VAR.P, and CORREL to analyze data trends, calculate standard deviation, variance, and correlation.

Example of calculating standard deviation:

```
StandardDeviation = STDEV.P(Sales[SalesAmount])
```

In this example, the STDEV.P function is used to calculate the standard deviation of sales amounts.

12.2 Forecasting and predictive analytics:

This section explores techniques for implementing forecasting and predictive analytics using DAX. It covers functions like FORECAST.ETS and PREDICT to generate forecasts and make predictions based on historical data.

Example of forecasting using exponential smoothing:

```
SalesForecast   =   FORECAST.ETS(Sales[SalesAmount],
Dates[Date], 12, "AAN")
```

In this example, the FORECAST.ETS function is used to generate a sales forecast for the next 12 periods using exponential smoothing with additive seasonality.

13 Advanced Data Modeling

13.1 Advanced data modeling techniques:

This chapter delves into advanced data modeling techniques in Power BI. It covers topics like bidirectional relationships, disconnected tables, and advanced filtering techniques.

Example of a bidirectional relationship:

```
Orders[OrderID] <-> OrderDetails[OrderID]
```

In this example, a bidirectional relationship is established between the Orders and OrderDetails tables, allowing filtering in both directions.

13.2 Implementing dynamic security:

This section explores implementing dynamic security in Power BI to control data access based on user roles and permissions. It covers techniques like row-level security (RLS) and user-based filtering.

Example of row-level security:

```
Sales[CustomerID]                            =
USERELATIONSHIP(Sales[CustomerID],
Users[CustomerID])
```

In this example, row-level security is implemented to restrict access to the Sales table based on the relationship between the CustomerID column in the Sales table and the CustomerID column in the Users table.

14 Advanced Data Transformations

14.1 Advanced data transformation techniques:

This chapter focuses on advanced data transformation techniques in Power Query Editor. It covers topics like conditional transformations, custom functions, and advanced merging and appending.

Example of conditional transformations:

```
= Table.AddColumn(Source, "DiscountedPrice", each if
[Quantity] > 10 then [Price] * 0.9 else [Price])
```

In this example, a conditional transformation is applied to add a DiscountedPrice column to the table. If the Quantity is greater than 10, the Price is discounted by 10%.

14.2 Creating custom functions:

This section explores the creation and usage of custom functions in Power Query Editor. It covers scenarios where built-in transformations may not suffice and custom logic is required.

Example of a custom function:

```
let
```

```
    DiscountedPrice = (price, quantity) => if quantity
> 10 then price * 0.9 else price,
        DiscountedTable  =  Table.AddColumn(Source,
"DiscountedPrice",  each  DiscountedPrice([Price],
[Quantity]))
in
    DiscountedTable
```

In this example, a custom function named DiscountedPrice is created and used to calculate the DiscountedPrice column based on the Price and Quantity columns.

15 Advanced Visualizations and Reporting

15.1 Custom visualizations using DAX expressions:

This chapter explores techniques for creating custom visualizations using DAX expressions. It covers the usage of functions like EVALUATE and ROW to generate custom tables and charts.

Example of a custom visualization using EVALUATE and ROW:

```
EVALUATE ROW("TotalSales", SUM(Sales[SalesAmount]))
```

In this example, a custom visualization is created using the EVALUATE and ROW functions to display the total sales amount.

15.2 Advanced reporting with bookmarks and drillthrough:

This section focuses on advanced reporting features like bookmarks and drillthrough. It covers techniques for creating interactive reports with bookmarked states and enabling drillthrough capabilities.

Example of using bookmarks to create interactive reports:

```
CreateBookmark("Summary", "SalesSummary", "Chart1",
"Table1")
```

In this example, a bookmark named "Summary" is created, capturing the current state of the report, including the selected chart and table visuals.

These examples and explanations provide a glimpse into the topics covered in each chapter, showcasing the practical application of advanced DAX techniques in Power BI.

16 Advanced Calculation Techniques

16.1 Dynamic calculation selection based on user input:

This chapter explores techniques to dynamically select calculations based on user input or parameters. It covers scenarios where the calculation logic needs to be adjusted dynamically.

Example of dynamic calculation selection based on user input:

```
SelectedCalculation =
    SWITCH(
        SELECTEDVALUE('CalculationSelector'[Calcula
tion]),
        "TotalSales", [TotalSales],
        "ProfitMargin", [ProfitMargin],
        "CustomCalculation", [CustomCalculation]
    )
```

In this example, the SWITCH function is used to dynamically select a calculation based on the value selected in a CalculationSelector table.

16.2 Advanced iterator functions for complex calculations:

This section focuses on advanced iterator functions like SUMMARIZE, SUMX, and AVERAGEX. It covers their usage in complex calculations involving multiple tables and aggregations.

Example of complex calculation using SUMMARIZE and SUMX:

```
TotalSalesByProduct =
SUMX(
        SUMMARIZE(Products,   Products[ProductID],
Products[ProductName]),
    [TotalSales]
)
```

In this example, the SUMMARIZE function is used to create a summary table of products, and then the SUMX function is used to calculate the total sales for each product.

16.3   Advanced filtering techniques using CALCULATE:

This subsection explores advanced filtering techniques using the CALCULATE function. It covers scenarios where complex filtering logic is required based on multiple conditions.

Example of advanced filtering using CALCULATE:

```
FilteredSalesAmount =
CALCULATE(
    SUM(Sales[SalesAmount]),
    Sales[Region] = "North",
    Sales[Year] = 2022,
    Sales[ProductCategory] = "Electronics"
)
```

In this example, the CALCULATE function is used to filter the Sales table based on specific conditions such as Region, Year, and ProductCategory, and then calculate the sum of SalesAmount.

17 Advanced DAX Formulas for Business Cases

In this chapter, we will explore a collection of advanced DAX formulas that are not commonly found in books but are highly relevant to solving complex business cases. These formulas will enable you to tackle real-world scenarios and provide valuable insights for decision-making.

17.1 Advanced Statistical Calculations

Example   1:   Calculating   Correlation   Coefficient

```
Correlation Coefficient =
VAR X = SUM(Data[Value_X])
VAR Y = SUM(Data[Value_Y])
VAR XY = SUMX(Data, Data[Value_X] * Data[Value_Y])
VAR XX = SUMX(Data, Data[Value_X]^2)
VAR YY = SUMX(Data, Data[Value_Y]^2)
VAR N = COUNTROWS(Data)

RETURN
(N * XY - X * Y) / SQRT((N * XX - X^2) * (N * YY - Y^2))
```

17.2 Advanced Financial Analysis

Example 2: Net Present Value (NPV) Calculation

```
NPV =
```

```
VAR CashFlows = VALUES(Data[CashFlow])
VAR DiscountRate = 0.1  // Assuming a discount rate
of 10%
VAR NPVValue =
    SUMX(
        CashFlows,
          [CashFlow] / (1 + DiscountRate)^([Year] -
MIN(Data[Year]))
    )
RETURN
    NPVValue
```

17.3 Advanced Customer Analytics

Example 3: Customer Segmentation using RFM (Recency, Frequency, Monetary) Analysis

```
RFM_Segment =
VAR RecencyScore = [Recency] // Calculate the Recency
score
VAR FrequencyScore = [Frequency] // Calculate the
Frequency score
VAR MonetaryScore = [Monetary] // Calculate the
Monetary score

RETURN
    RecencyScore * 100 + FrequencyScore * 10 +
MonetaryScore
```

17.4 Advanced Sales Analytics

Example 4: Sales Growth Rate Calculation

```
SalesGrowthRate =
VAR CurrentSales = SUM(Data[Sales])
VAR    PreviousSales    =    CALCULATE(SUM(Data[Sales]),
PREVIOUSMONTH(Data[Date]))

RETURN
          DIVIDE(CurrentSales    -    PreviousSales,
PreviousSales)
```

17.5 Advanced Supply Chain and Inventory Analysis

Example 5: Safety Stock Calculation

```
SafetyStock =
VAR AverageDemand = AVERAGE(Data[Demand])
VAR StandardDeviation = STDEV.P(Data[Demand])
VAR LeadTime = 7  // Assuming a lead time of 7 days
VAR ServiceLevel = 0.95 // Target service level of
95%
VAR ZScore = NORM.S.INV(ServiceLevel)

RETURN
     ZScore * StandardDeviation * SQRT(LeadTime) +
AverageDemand
```

17.6 Advanced Marketing Analytics

Example 6: Return on Investment (ROI) Calculation

```
ROI =
VAR MarketingCost = SUM(Data[MarketingCost])
VAR Revenue = SUM(Data[Revenue])

RETURN
    (Revenue - MarketingCost) / MarketingCost
```

17.7 Advanced HR Analytics

Example 7: Employee Attrition Rate Calculation

```
AttritionRate =
VAR                 EmployeesStart              =
CALCULATE(DISTINCTCOUNT(Data[EmployeeID]),
PREVIOUSYEAR(Data[Date]))
VAR EmployeesEnd = DISTINCTCOUNT(Data[EmployeeID])

RETURN
        DIVIDE(EmployeesEnd    -    EmployeesStart,
EmployeesStart)
```

17.8 Advanced Risk Analysis

Example 8: Value at Risk (VaR) Calculation

```
VaR =
VAR PortfolioValue = SUM(Data[PortfolioValue])
VAR Returns = Data[Returns]
VAR ConfidenceLevel = 0.95 // Desired confidence
level of 95%
VAR ZScore = NORM.S.INV(ConfidenceLevel)
```

```
VAR PortfolioReturns = SUMX(Returns, Returns)

RETURN
                PortfolioValue    *    ZScore    *
STDEV.P(PortfolioReturns)
```

18 Publishing and Sharing Power BI Reports

After you have completed your analysis and visualization work in Power BI Desktop, you will want to publish and share your reports to allow others to access your insights. Here is a step-by-step guide to publish and share Power BI reports.

18.1 Publish the Report

1. From Power BI Desktop, go to the Home tab and click on the "Publish"   button.

2. Power BI will ask you to save your changes if you haven't done so. Click "Save" to proceed.
3. You will be prompted to select the destination workspace in Power BI service (app.powerbi.com). If you haven't logged in, you will need to sign in with your Power BI account.
4. Select the workspace where you want to publish the report, then click "Select".

Once publishing is done, a success message will appear with an option to open the report in Power BI service.

18.2 Share the Report

1. Open the Power BI service in a web browser and log in if necessary.
2. Navigate to the workspace where you published your report.
3. Open the report you want to share.
4. Once your report is opened, click on the "Share" button at the top of the page.

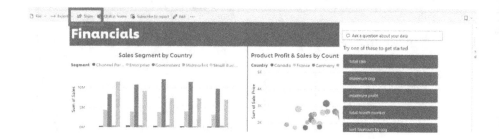

In the Share report window, you have the option to share the report via email. Simply enter the email addresses of the individuals with whom you wish to share the report.

You can also choose whether recipients can share the report with others, and whether they can build content like dashboards and reports based on your dataset.

After setting your preferences, click on the "Share" button.

18.3 Manage Permissions

To manage or review the permissions of the report, go to the Settings (gear icon) in Power BI service, then click on "Manage permissions".

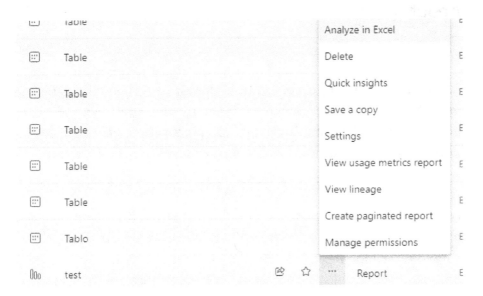

Here, you can add or remove individuals, change their access levels, and decide whether they can reshare the report.

Remember, you need the proper licenses to share your reports in Power BI service. Either you or the recipient(s) must have a Power BI Pro license, or the content needs to be in a workspace that's in a Premium capacity.

Lastly, always be mindful of the data you are sharing and ensure it adheres to your organization's policies on data security and privacy.

About Author

Ece Karakaş is a highly accomplished software engineer with expertise in Python and a broad range of other technologies. With a strong educational background and years of practical experience, Ece has become a trusted authority in the field of software development.

Ece holds a Bachelor's degree in Chemical Engineering and an MBA, providing a solid foundation in both technical and business aspects of software development. Her diverse skill set allows her to approach projects from a holistic perspective, ensuring that solutions are not only technically sound but also aligned with strategic business goals.

Throughout her career, Ece has worked on a variety of projects across industries such as finance, e-commerce, and telecommunications. She has successfully developed and delivered high-quality software solutions, leveraging the power of Python as well as other technologies like Power BI, RPA (Robotic Process Automation), and Power Automate.

Ece's expertise in Python goes beyond the basics. She has a natural curiosity for exploring advanced techniques and high-level tricks, constantly pushing the boundaries of what can be achieved with the language. Her deep understanding of Python allows her to solve complex problems efficiently and elegantly.

In addition to her technical expertise, Ece is a dedicated educator and mentor. She enjoys sharing her knowledge and helping others succeed in their software development journeys. Through online platforms and community engagements, she provides guidance and support to aspiring developers, inspiring them to excel in their Python programming endeavors.

Beyond Python, Ece possesses a wide-ranging skill set in other areas of software development. Her proficiency extends to technologies like Power BI, enabling her to create insightful data visualizations and analytics. She is also experienced in RPA, leveraging automation to streamline business processes, and Power Automate, empowering organizations to automate workflows and tasks.

Ece's commitment to staying updated with the latest trends and advancements in the industry ensures that she remains at the forefront of technology. She actively explores emerging technologies, incorporating them into her work to deliver innovative and forward-thinking solutions.

With her technical prowess, comprehensive expertise, and dedication to continuous learning, Ece Karakaş is a valuable resource for those looking to enhance their Python skills and develop robust software solutions. Her passion for technology, combined with her ability to bridge technical and business domains, makes her an invaluable asset in the field of software development.